The Guidefa...

A three part, easy to follow, informa...
preparing for your baby, caring for y... ...
you ready for the change from tot to toddler.

Become a 'man of honor'

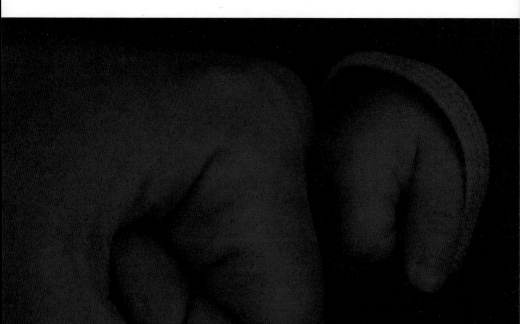

The Guidefather

Contents

There's a first for everything!

'Information you can't refuse'

An information guide that will give you the essentials in caring for your child from 0 - 2 years old.

The Guidefather has been divided into three parts.
'The Guidefather trilogy'

Part I

The Essentials

Fail to prepare
prepare to fail

page 2 - 15

This section includes all the essentials to get you started in order to care for your baby. Product information and quantity of each essential needed has been provided to give you a head start.

Part II

Baby's First Everyday Care

0 - 6
Months

page 16 - 90

This section includes information about your baby and how to care for your baby, once he or she has arrived. This part provides easy to follow, step-by-step diagrams and information, from preparation, to practice, to then becoming a pro.

Part III

From Baby To Toddler

6 Months
plus

page 91 - 127

This section includes information about your baby's transition from baby to toddler. From six to twenty four months your baby will learn, grow and develop, this part will prepare you for those changes.

Part I
The essentials

Capisce! *(Understand)*

Baby Grooming

What you'll need...

Small bath tub
Amount: 1
Small bath tub used for bathing your baby before they are at the age of using an adult bath assisted with a bath seat.

Hooded towels
Amount: 2 - 3
Hooded towels are used to pat your baby dry after their bath. The hood is ideal for drying hair and keeping your baby warm.

Wash cloths
Amount: 2 - 3
Used for cleaning your baby during bath time or nappy change.

Dental care
Amount: 1
Gauze and children's fluoride toothpaste can be used to clean your baby's gums/teeth. Once their teeth have fully grown a children's tooth brush can be used.

Shampoo
Amount: 1
Use shampoo designed for babies.

Soap
Amount: 1
Use soap designed for babies.

Nasal bulb
Amount: 1
Used for cleaning your baby's nose.

Wipes
Amount: 1 Multi-pack
Can be used for cleaning your baby from birth. Water wipes recommended.

Petroleum jelly
Amount: 1 Tub
Used on dry skin to keep lubricated.

Nappy cream
Amount: 1
To treat nappy rash. It can be purchased over the counter or can be recommended to you by a health care professional or pharmacist.

Lotion
Amount: 1
Can be applied after bath time, it can be massaged into their skin to help them relax and sleep.

Grooming kit
Amount: 1
Most include, nail scissors, nail file and baby brush/comb.

Cotton pads
Amount: 1 Multi-pack
Used with warm water to clean your baby.

Disposable nappies
Amount: 1 - 2 Packs
Disposable nappies are discarded after they are used. They are easy and quick to apply.

Waste nappy bags
Amount: 1 Box
Used to dispose dirty nappies, helps to minimise odours.

Small cups or bowls
Amount: Selection
Can be used while bathing your baby. Ideal for rinsing off baby soap or shampoo.

Baby bath seat
Amount: 1
Can be used once your baby is sitting up unaided, it will prevent your baby from slipping in the bath.

Baby changing mat
Amount: 2
A thicker foam changing mat can be used at home. A thinner cushioned changing mat which can fold or roll, is ideal to be placed into your changing bag.

Thermometer
Amount: 1
The easiest way to checking your baby's temperature. Always use thermometer under armpit.

Baby Clothing

What you'll need...

Baby grows
Amount: 5-7
Can be used for both day and night.

Cardigans
Amount: 2
Preferably wool or cotton rather than nylon material. Light weight rather than heavy.

Vests
Amount: 3-5
Helps to keep your baby warm.

Bibs
Amount: 3-5
To be used when feeding your baby.

Mittens
Amount: 3-5
Helps keep hands warm as well as protecting your baby from scratching themselves. Close knitted patterns are best so that your baby's fingers will not get caught.

Hats
Amount: 2-3
Helps to keep your baby warm. Prevents heat escaping through your baby's head.

Socks
Amount: 2-3 pairs
Helps to keep your baby's feet warm. Close knitted patterns are best so that your baby's toes will not get caught.

Jacket/Coat
Amount: 1-2
Used for layering during the colder months, keeping your baby warm.

Grow bag
Amount: 1
For when your baby sleeps, these have been designed to be used as a safer alternative to blankets.

CAUTION:
Washing powders/fabric softeners must always be fragrance free and chemical free.
Always rinse clothing thoroughly.

Baby Bedding

What you'll need...

Moses basket
Amount: 1

A moses basket is a portable bed, that has a firm well fitted mattress and comes with a sturdy stand. This must be used for the first few months.

Cot
Amount: 1

Your baby's cot must be sturdy, the cot bars must be smooth, and distance between no less than 25mm and no more than 60mm. Moving parts should work smoothly. Never leave anything with ties in the cot, e.g bibs. Cot bumpers are not recommended.

Cot mattress
Amount: 1

Must be firm and fit snuggly with no gaps around the edges of the cot.

Sheets
Amount: 3-5

Sheets need to be changed often. Using fitted sheets makes life a lot easier.

Light blankets
Amount: Selection

Light blankets can be used when layering your baby to keep them warm.

Pillow
Amount: 2

CAUTION:
Do not use until 1 year old.

Night light
Amount: 1

Used to comfort your baby during the night. Also gives you enough light for night feeds without fully awakening your baby.

Room thermostat
Amount: 1

Used to monitor the temperature of the room your baby is in. Make sure the room has a temperature between 16 and 20 degrees, ideal for their safety and comfort.

Out & About

What you'll need...

Pushchair
Amount: 1
Lightweight and collapsible. Ideal for taking with you when going away on holiday.

Pram
Amount: 1
Gives your baby a lot of space to sit and lie comfortably however keep in mind, it may take up a lot of space. Look for one that can be dismantled easily.

TOP TIP!
Always test drive pushchairs and prams before you buy. Make sure breaks are in good working order and frame is strong enough.

Carry cot
Amount: 1
Light and portable with handles. Often attachable to a wheeled frame and some can be taken into a car with appropriate restraints. Your baby can sleep for a few hours in a carry cot for the first few months.

Car seat
Amount: 1
If you have a car, you must have a car seat which your baby must always travel in. It is illegal to travel without one. The best way for your baby to travel is either on the front or back seat in a rear facing infant car seat, which must be held in place by the adult safety belt.

CAUTION:
Do not place car seat in the front passenger seat if your car is fitted with an air bag. Do not buy a second hand car seat as it may have previously been damaged in an accident. Always ensure the car seat is fitted correctly.

Baby carrier
Amount: 1
Must be carried in front of you for the first four months. Babies like to be close and warm to you.

Baby changing bag
Amount: 1
A must have for storing all of your baby's essentials needed for when you are out and about.

TOP TIP!
Think about what will suit you best. Consider weight and size.

Baby feeding

What you'll need...

Bottles
Amount: 2-3
There are a variety of bottles and teats available in different shapes and sizes, a simple easy to clean bottle is best.

Steriliser
Amount: 1
There are several ways in which you can sterilise the equipment.
1- Cold water sterilise solution.
2- Steam sterilising.
3- Sterilising by boiling.

Formula
Amount: 2 - 3
Formula is available in two forms. Ready to feed liquid formula, sold in cartons which is sterile, or powdered formula which is not sterile.

Muslin cloth
Amount: 6-12
A muslin cloth can be used when burping your baby as well as a comforter for your baby.

Pacifier/Dummy
Amount: 1 pack
A pacifier can help soothe your baby when crying, as well as help comfort them while making a feed.

Baby high chair
Amount: 1
Can be used when your baby can sit up unaided, it will limit their mobility and movement to make it easier when feeding.

CAUTION:
Although a pacifier can be used to soothe your baby between feeding, it must never replace a feed.

CAUTION:
Never leave your baby unattended in their high chair.

Baby cutlery set 6 Months+
Amount: 1-2 sets
Needs to be child friendly, it is used when weaning your baby onto solid foods and when they are learning to feed themselves.

Partners Breast pump
Amount: 1
A device which allows mothers to express breast milk. Perfect for allowing fathers to take part in the feeding process.

Extras

What you'll need...

Teething rings
Amount: 1-2

These are safe for your baby to chew on while teething, the bright colours and textures captivate your baby and can also be fun to rattle.

Teething gel
Amount: 1

Used on babies over four months old. Is sugar free and contains a mild local anaesthetic which helps to numb your baby's gums.

TOP TIP!
Can be cooled in the fridge to help soothe baby's gums. (Not freezer)

No-spill cup 1year+
Amount: 2 - 3

This is ideal because it has a lid that cannot release liquid without suction, if dropped it will not spill.

Medicine
Amount: 1

Can be used if your baby is in pain or has a raised temperature. Specially designed for children that contains a small dose of paracetamol or ibuprofen.

Potty
Amount: 2 - 3

This can be used as well as a toilet training seat. Having a few around the house is ideal to avoid any mishaps. Taking one on holiday or on car journeys is essential.

Toilet training seat
Amount: 1

Placed on top of your standard toilet seat, it is the perfect size for your toddler. Most have cushion padding to make it more comfortable, this gets them used to using a toilet.

Toilet step
Amount: 1

Used to make it easier for your toddler to step up and onto a standard toilet. It can also be used to step up and reach the sink when brushing teeth.

Pull up pants
Amount: 1 pack

Used before big kid pants, they are like underwear but have protection in case of any accidents.

Big kid pants
Amount: 1 pack
These can help encourage your toddler to stop wearing nappies or pull ups, it will make them feel grown up and as if they have accomplished something.

Hand soap/sanitiser
Amount: 1
Quick and easy to use to ensure your hands are always clean.

Waterproof mattress sheets
Amount: 1 pack
This will protect your baby's mattress in case they wet the bed during the night.

Toy box
Amount: 1
Playing with toys is not only fun, but one of the most effective ways to help your baby to learn. A variety of toys in their toy box will keep your baby interested.

Sun lotion
Amount: 1
To be applied when your baby's skin is exposed to the sun. An essential for summer time and holidays.

TOP TIP!
Apply sun lotion 30 minutes prior to sun exposure.

Monitor
Amount: 1
A device that transmits sounds made by your baby for you to hear or see while in another room. Always keep the monitor close to your baby's cot.

Formula maker
Amount: 1
This machine is a formula mixer and dispenser. It prepares accurate measurments for feeds at the right temperature quick and easy, at a push of a button.

Books
Amount: Multiple
Important for helping your baby and toddler develop. Reading your baby books and showing them pictures will help them with learning and speech.

Checklists
Be prepared

These checklists will ensure you have everything you'll need for when your baby arrives, not only for yourself but also for your baby and partner.

Labour bags will be used when your baby arrives. The changing bag is used everyday to carry everything you'll need for your baby.

The following lists have been provided for your reference.

Baby's Labour Bag

Dad's Labour Bag

Mother's Labour Bag

Changing Bag

For your baby

Hand sanitizer gel

2x Dummies/pacifiers

2x Bibs

2x Muslin cloths

Changing mat

Nappies (new born and 1 size up)

Nappy bags
(scented recommended)

Cotton wool pads

Baby wipes
(water wipes recommended)

Nappy cream

2x Vests

2x Baby grows/onesie

2x Pair of socks

Mittens

Baby hat

2x Blankets

Jacket

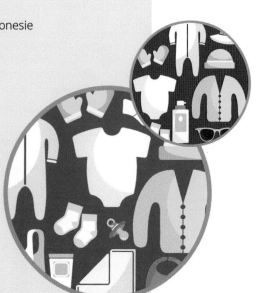

For yourself

Snacks

Energy drinks/glucose tablets

Mobile phone
(with charger)

Tablet
(with charger)

Coins for parking and
vending machines

Deodorant

Mens cologne

Toothbrush and toothpaste

Change of clothes

Special present and card
for your partner

 TOP TIP!
Install baby car seat before
baby's arrival

For your partner

Maternity notes

Birth plan

Night dress (for labour)

Pyjamas/night dress
(after labour)

Outfit (for going home)

Underwear

Socks

Slippers

Dressing gown

Towels

Toiletries

Toothbrush and toothpaste

Hair brush and hair
bands/clips

Lip balm

Maternity sanitary pads

Breast feeding/nursing bras

Breast pads

Nipple shields

Nipple cream

Snacks

Energy/glucose tablets

Bottled water

Books and magazines

Tablet (with charger)

Mobile phone (with charger)

The Changing Bag

For yourself

Keys

Wallet

Mobile phone

Snacks

Bottle of water

Hand sanitizer gel

Baby clothing

Vest

Onesie/baby grow

Cardigan or sweater

Socks

Mittens

Winter hat

Sun hat

Sun lotion

For Feeding
(depending on breast feeding or formula feeding)

Bottle of expressed breast milk

Carton of ready-made formula milk

Canister of milk powder

Bottle of pre-boiled water

2x sterilised bottles

For Baby

Your baby's medical notes

2x dummies/pacifiers

2x bibs

2x muslin cloths

Changing mat

Nappies

Nappy bags
(scented recommended)

Cotton wool pads

Baby wipes
(water wipes recommended)

Nappy cream

Paracetamol liquid sachets/medicine (if needed)

Colic relief (if needed)

Teething gel (if needed)

Teething ring (if needed)

Soft toys and rattles

Part II
Bada bing
bada boom

Congratulations, your
baby has arrived!

Baby's first - Everyday Care

Your Bambino

1 Anterior Fontanelle
- SOFT SPOT!
Where the bone of your baby's skull has not yet grown together.
It should seal by the end of the first year.

2 Posterior Fontanelle
- SOFT SPOT!
Where the bone of your baby's skull has not yet grown together.
It should seal by the end of the first year.

3 Downy coating will disappear within weeks.

4 Skin: Soft and sensitive to harsh chemicals. Also 15 times thinner than an adults.

5 Umbilical stump:
Will start to scab, turn black and will fall off eventually. Always keep clean and dry.

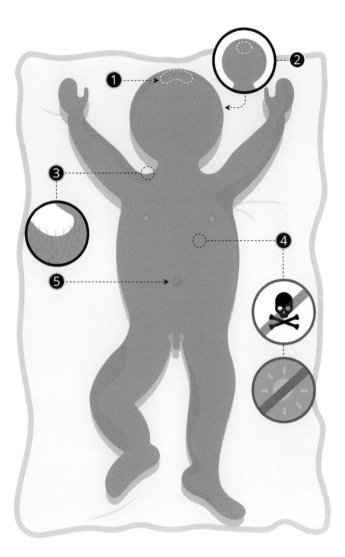

Baby progression stages

Here are the stages of a baby's progression.
All babies are unique and your baby's progression may be slightly different than shown.

Birth - 1 Month
Smile

1- 3 Months
Respond to affection

3 - 6 Months
Roll over

6 - 9 Months
Sit up

9 - 12 Months
Crawl

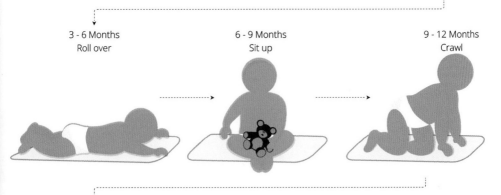

12 - 18 Months
Stand

12 - 24 Months
Walk

2 - 3 Years
Talk

Ciao!

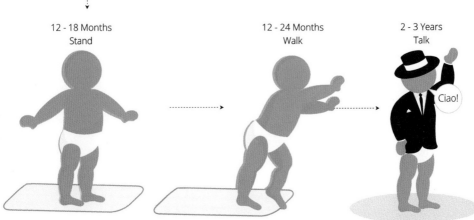

Handling your baby

Always ensure your hands are clean before handling your baby. If you can't access soap and water, disinfect your hands by using hand santiser or clean with baby wipes.

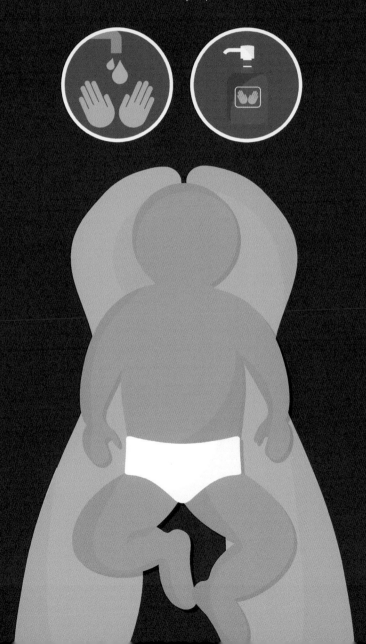

19

Picking up your baby

For some of you, this may be the first time handling a baby.

Always ensure your baby's head and neck is supported at all times before lifting.

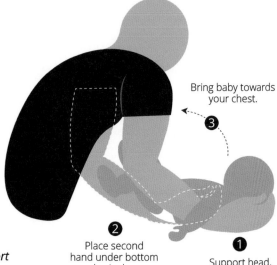

Bring baby towards your chest.

3

2 Place second hand under bottom and spinal area.

1 Support head, slide hand under neck and head.

CAUTION:
Until your baby's neck strengthens, always support it, this will help to prevent undesirable flopping.

TOP TIP!
Placing your baby's head on your chest so that they are close to you, will help soothe and relax them.

CAUTION:
When laying your baby down always support their head and ensure that the surface will also support your baby's head and neck.

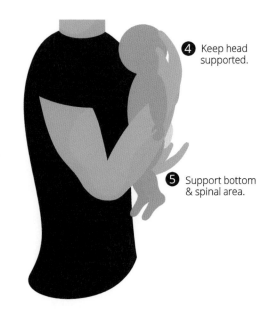

4 Keep head supported.

5 Support bottom & spinal area.

The Cradle Hold

The cradle hold is an ideal hold when needing to perform other tasks with your free hand. Baby's head and neck should be supported by the bend of your arm.

TOP TIP:
By cradling your baby with its head on the left side of your body, the rhythmic thumping produced by your heart beat will help comfort your baby and may put them to sleep.

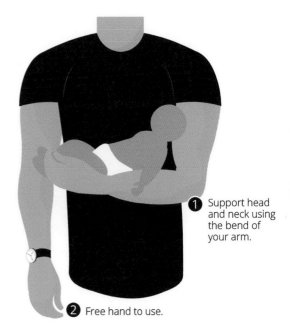

1 Support head and neck using the bend of your arm.

2 Free hand to use.

The Shoulder Hold

An ideal hold for comforting your baby as there is enough support to rock or sway.

1 Baby's head should rest on the front of your shoulder.

3 Keep your free hand on your baby's back / head for extra support and a more secure hold.

2 Use the bend of your arm to support baby's bottom.

TOP TIP!
If you lean forward remember to support your baby's head and neck.

Passing & receiving your baby

This ensures a safe technique for passing your baby.

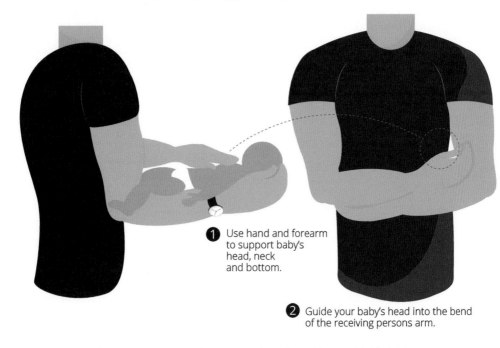

1 Use hand and forearm to support baby's head, neck and bottom.

2 Guide your baby's head into the bend of the receiving persons arm.

TOP TIP!
Make sure the person who is receiving your baby has clean hands.

Show me some love

Comforting your baby

Get prepared:
Comforting

There are various techniques you can perform to help comfort your baby. Some may be more effective than others.

Pacifier/Dummie

Muslin cloth

Pram

Toys

Sway to comfort

Hold your baby close to you, gently bounce and sway side to side while talking or singing to your baby. This will soothe your baby, however sometimes it may keep your baby awake, laying them down can help.

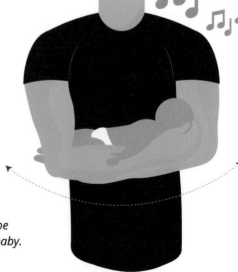

CAUTION:
The bouncing motion should be gentle to avoid shaking your baby.

Rock to comfort

Place your baby in a pushchair or pram, go for a walk or rock them back and forth, the steady and smooth rhythm will soothe your baby. An alternative way of rocking is to sit in a rocking chair when holding your baby.

Baby comforters

Your baby may find comfort in sucking on a sterilised dummie as well as using a muslin cloth as a comforter. Your baby may also find their own thumb or your finger instead of a dummie.

CAUTION:

If your baby uses your hand or finger to pacify themselves, ensure that your hands are always clean.

Do not tie a dummie to your baby with a cord or string, this may be a choking and strangulation hazard.

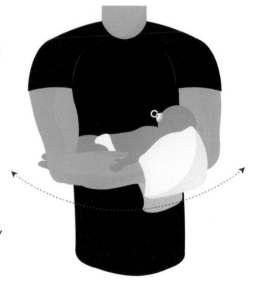

Massage to comfort

Massage has a calming effect on most babies. It also allows you to develop a closer bond with your child.

Make sure the room is warm enough, undress your baby and massage them with baby oil using gentle stroking movements.

TOP TIP!
Massage classes are available with more in-depth massage techniques.

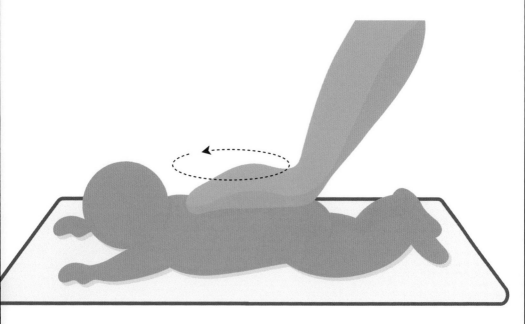

Dirty business

The nappy change

Get prepared: Changing station setup

Have your nappy changing station set up and ready to use, it will make nappy changing much easier, having everything you need at hand.

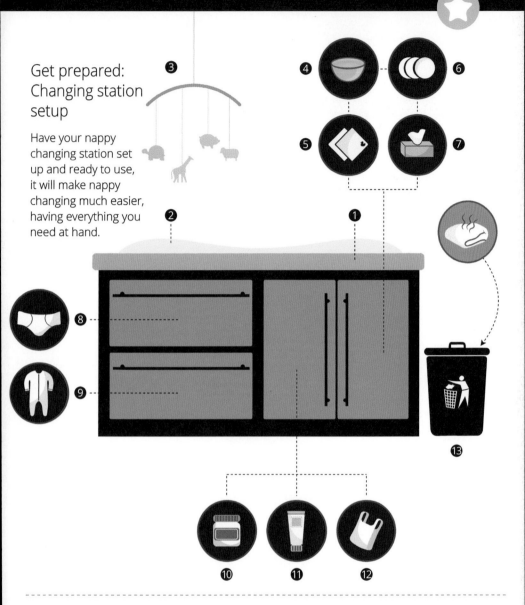

1. Changing table (A few inches above waist level)
2. Foam changing cushion or changing mat
3. Mobile entertainment (To occupy your baby)
4. Bowl (For warm water)
5. Wash cloths
6. Cotton pads x 12+
7. Baby wipes - water wipes can be used from birth
8. Nappies x 12+
9. Extra clothes (In case of a messy emergency)
10. Petroleum jelly
11. Creams
12. Nappy bags
13. Bin (Empty frequently)

Nappy removal

Check to see if your baby has a wet or dirty nappy, most nappies have a wetness indicator on them, otherwise this can be checked by gently inserting your finger into the side of the nappy to feel for wetness or through smell for a dirty nappy.

Frequent nappy changing will help to avoid nappy rash.

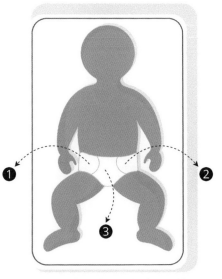

Unfasten and peel away the front of the nappy in order of 1-2-3.

Cleaning your baby

Clean your baby by using a bowl of clean warm water and cotton pads and follow steps 1 to 3.

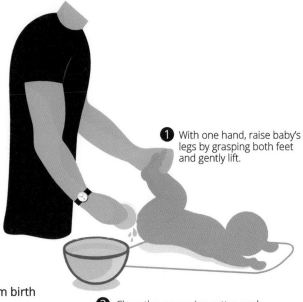

1 With one hand, raise baby's legs by grasping both feet and gently lift.

TOP TIP!
Wipes can be used from birth but must be water wipes.

2 Clean the area using cotton pads and warm water.

Once area is dry apply the new fresh nappy.

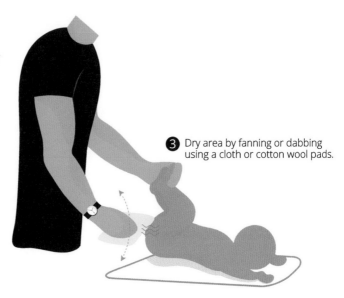

3 Dry area by fanning or dabbing using a cloth or cotton wool pads.

Changing your baby boy

If your baby has a dirty nappy use clean edge of nappy to wipe away any faeces from baby's skin.

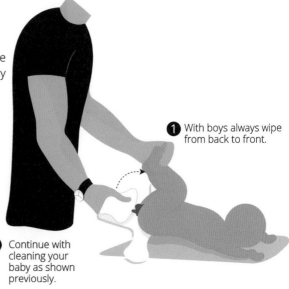

1 With boys always wipe from back to front.

2 Continue with cleaning your baby as shown previously.

CAUTION:
Be careful... he might sprinkle his tinkle! To prevent this, place wash cloth over the area.

Changing your baby Girl

If your baby has a dirty nappy use clean edge of nappy to wipe away any faeces from baby's skin.

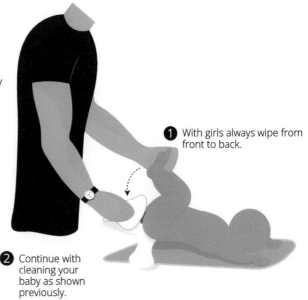

1 With girls always wipe from front to back.

2 Continue with cleaning your baby as shown previously.

Applying a fresh nappy

First, open a fresh nappy and place it underneath your baby with fastening tabs at the rear.

Apply as shown in the diagram.

TOP TIP!
Make sure the nappy fits snugly but not too tightly around your baby's stomach.

CAUTION:
Do not cover umbilical stump fold down the front of nappy 1 - 2 inches before fastening.

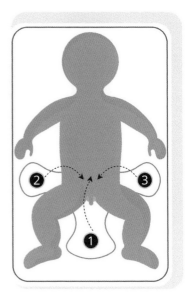

Apply nappy in order of 1-2-3 securing each fastener.

Dirty nappy colour guide

This colour guide will help you identify the difference between a healthy and unhealthy stool. Checking the colour of your baby's stool will help you indicate any signs of illness.

Colour:
Greenish-black

Appearance:
Licorice colour or sticky tar.

What does it mean?
This is the meconium stool which is the first that your baby will have- after birth. It is perfectly normal and will pass after around three days as receiving feedings will move this through their system.

What should I do?
It is normal, healthy and temporary, but if it lasts more than three days, check with your doctor.

Colour:
Greenish-brown

Appearance:
Leftover guacamole.

What does it mean?
This is a normal stool when your baby starts eating solids.

What should I do?
This is a normal and healthy stool. If it appears before introducing solids, it is usually normal but if your baby has other symptoms that concern you, contact your health care professional.

Colour:
Yellow and seedy

Appearance:
Yellow, curdled milk.

What does it mean?
This is breast fed baby stools, which is normal with a mild smell and will- continue to appear this colour until you supplement with formula or begin feeding your baby solid foods.

What should I do?
It is a standard stool and shows your baby is getting the ideal nutrients from breast milk to stay healthy and grow strong.

Colour:
Tan

Appearance:
Thick hummus.

What does it mean?
This is formula fed baby's stools which is normal unless it becomes hard (small hard balls) or is watery.

What should I do?
This is a standard stool, and is normal and healthy. If stools are hard or watery, contact your health care professional.

Dirty nappy colour guide

Colour:
Brown

Appearance:
Watery and loose with chunks.

What does it mean?
An occasional loose stool is normal however if it occurs regularly for two days or more it could be diarrhea- which can be a sign of infection. Although the infection may not be dangerous diarrhea can cause dehydration.

What should I do?
If this persists for more than two days, contact your health care professional. Do not give your baby anti-diarrhea medication unless advised.

Colour:
Dark Brown

Appearance:
Dry and hard like pebbles.

What does it mean?
A hard stool can cause constipation. An occasional hard stool is normal, especially with formula fed babies and when introducing solids. However can be a sign of your baby not getting enough fluids.

What should I do?
Consult your health care professional if your baby is very young. Older babies can be given plenty to drink and if eating solids should be given foods higher in fiber, such as, fruits, vegetables and whole grains.

Colour:
Pinkish-red

Appearance:
Partially digested foods.

What does it mean?
These stools occur once your baby has started on solids, they will vary in colour and texture after every meal. Some medication can also turn stools unusual colours.

What should I do?
Ensure there is a link to the colour of the stool and what your baby is eating. E.g carrots - orange stools. If your baby's stool is red for no apparent reason contact your health care professional.

Colour:
Dark green

Appearance:
Thick, dark stool.

What does it mean?
This colour stool is caused from iron sulfate in a supplement in your baby's diet.

What should I do?
This is normal. Iron supplementation does not cause digestive problems or discomfort.

Dirty nappy colour guide

Colour:
Bright green

Appearance:
Green, frothy stools.

What does it mean?
Breast fed babies who receive more fore-milk (sweeter and thinner) than hind-milk (richer and fattier) sometimes have bright green stools. If your baby has a virus it can turn their stool bright green.

What should I do?
Your baby may need to nurse for longer on each side to ensure enough hind-milk is consumed during each feed. If your baby produces this colour stool and seems fussy or uncomfortable contact your health care professional as it may be a virus.

Colour:
Red-streaked

Appearance:
Hard stool, streaked with blood or mucus.

What does it mean?
Bright red blood often occurs in stools of constipated babies which indicates that they may have small tears/cracks- around the anus caused by pushing.

What should I do?
If your doctor confirms that the bleeding is from the small tears/cracks it should disappear once constipation has passed. If there is a large amount of blood or the bleeding does not disappear when the stools have softened, contact your health care professional.

Colour:
Chalky white

Appearance:
Pale, colourless stool.

What does it mean?
Might be a sign of a liver or gallbladder problem from lack of bile which normally turns a stool brown.

What should I do?
This is very rare but if it occurs contact your health care professional right away.

Colour:
Black

Appearance:
Thick or tarry.

What does it mean?
Might contain blood that entered the intestine in the upper portion of the digestive system.

What should I do?
If this is not the meconium stool that passes during the first few days of life, contact your health professional immediately.

Nappy rash

Nappy rash is an inflammatory condition caused by sensitive skin, rubbing, chafing or from using soaps/baby wipes. The easiest way to prevent it, is to change nappies often.

How to treat

1 Use cotton wool pads and warm water to clean.

2 Avoid excessive wiping, rather use patting motions to clean.

3 Always allow your baby to air-dry properly. Leaving the nappy off for as long as possible, allowing fresh air to get to the skin.

4 A mild ointment can be applied.

Skin may appear red with small bumps.

TOP TIP!
If a rash occurs, avoid using wipes, as they contain alcohol which may aggravate the rash.

CAUTION:
If the inflamed area has blisters, your baby may have a underlying fungal infection.
- Consult your doctor

If the inflamed area is surrounded by red dots, your baby may have a yeast infection.
- Consult your doctor

Leave the cannoli take the bottle

Feeding your baby

Get prepared:
Breastfeeding

Ideally babies should be breast fed for around the first six months. Any amount of breastfeeding has a positive effect.

Breast pump

Breastfeeding is the healthiest way to feed your baby because there are many benefits. If your baby is being breast fed, as a father, there are other ways that you can bond with your baby. Have your partner express the breast milk into a bottle, for you to feed them. Have skin to skin contact with your baby laying against your chest, allowing them to listen to the deep, relaxing rumble of your voice.

In the first few days after birth a fluid is produced called colostrum. It is a golden yellow colour and very concentrated food. It contains antibodies to protect the newborn against disease.

Newborn babies will want to feed often, sometimes every hour. After a few days, once more 'mature' milk starts to produce, your baby's feeds will start to become fewer and longer.

Antinatal classes are available to learn about positioning and attachment, expressing breast milk and problems that may occur when your partner is breastfeeding.

Breast milk	
🙂 Pros	Cons
It is free.	Mother may feel 'tied' to the baby.
Always available.	More frequent feedings.
Natural method of feeding.	Father may feel left out.
Supplies antibodies.	Cannot measure food intake.
May lower risk of SIDS (sudden infant death syndrome)	

Get prepared:
Formula feeding

The amount of formula your baby will consume will vary. Newborn babies will consume a small amount to start with. Most will need 150 - 200ml per kilo of their weight per day. This may fluctuate depending on health, growth spurts, activity and even outdoor weather conditions. Feed your baby when they show signs of wanting food.

After the first week your baby may lose up to one-tenth of their birth weight. An indication that your baby is getting enough formula will be weight gain and the number of wet and dirty nappies they produce. Your baby will require fewer feeding's as they age.

Bottles

Steriliser

Formula

Muslin cloth

Bibs

TOP TIP!
Feeding your baby out and about can be made easier by taking a measured amount of formula in a small, clean, dry container. A vacuum flask of hot boiled water and a sterilised bottle with cap.

Formula milk

😊 Pros	Cons 😞
Can be fed by anyone.	No antibodies in formula.
Can measure food intake.	Can be expensive.
Fewer feeding required.	More equipment required.
Night time feedings can be shared.	More preparation.

Hunger reflex

To test if your baby is hungry, stroke your baby's cheek with your finger. If their mouth opens in the direction of your finger and they appear to be searching for food, this means that they are hungry.

Another indication that they are hungry may be sucking on your hand or their own fingers.

Expressed breast milk storing

If your partner is breast feeding your baby, always store the expressed breast milk in a sterilised container and place it into your fridge for up to five days at 4°C or lower.

Freezing breast milk

You may also want to freeze your partners expressed breast milk and it is safe to do so by storing it in the freezer compartment of your fridge for up to six months.

Defrosting and warming

Defrost the expressed breast milk in the fridge. Once defrosted use straight away. It can be consumed cool or warmed by placing the bottle into a bowl of luke warm water.

Do not use a microwave for heating, as it will cause hot spots.

 CAUTION:
Do not re-heat your baby's milk.
Do not re-freeze milk once it has thawed.

Preparing for a feed

Sterilising feeding equipment is very important. This should be done between each feed.

There are several ways to sterilise your baby's feeding equipment.

- Cold water sterilising solution
- Steam sterilising.
- Sterilising by boiling.

TOP TIP!
The best way to reduce risk of infection from bacteria is to make up one feed at a time.

CAUTION:
It is important to follow the manufacturers instructions for the certain type of steriliser you own as they may differ.

Always throw away unused formula.

Steam sterilising show below

1
Using hot soapy water, clean bottle and teats using a clean bottle brush.

2
Rinse using clean, cold running water.

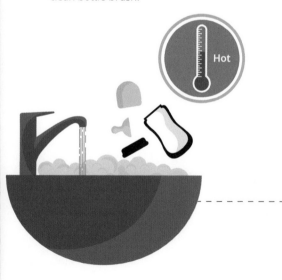

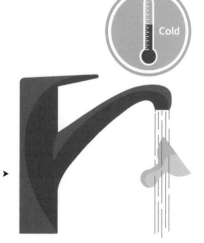

❸
Place equipment into steriliser, make sure the opening of bottles and teats are facing down.

❹
Rinse equipment in cold water, this will also help to cool it down.

Cold

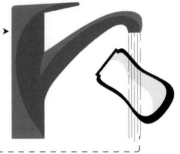

❺
Always use freshly boiled drinking water from the tap. Leave water to cool in the kettle for no longer than 30 minutes.

❻
While the water is still hot, pour correct amount into the bottle first and follow with the correct amount of infant formula. Follow manufactures instructions

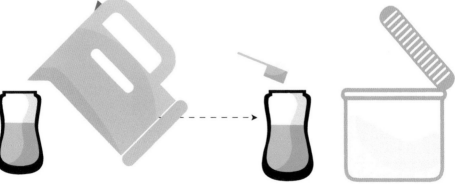

CAUTION:
Bottled water needs to be boiled in the same way as tap water, as it is not sterile.

Cover teat with cap, shake bottle until
powder has dissolved.
Let formula cool, test temperature of
formula on the inside of your wrist,
it should feel warm or cool.

If the formula is still too hot, run
the bottom of the bottle under
cold water avoid wetting the cap.
Test on wrist again.

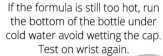

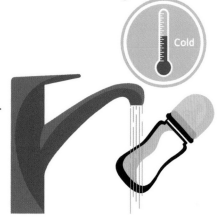

CAUTIONS!

Follow manufactures instructions very carefully.
Amount of water and powder will vary.

Do not add extra powder, as this can cause
constipation and dehydration. Do not add too
little powder as it may not provide your baby
with enough nourishment.

Never warm formula in a microwave as it will
heat unevenly and may burn your baby's mouth.

Never pour boiling water while holding your baby.
A baby's skin is fifteen times thinner than an adults.

Feeding your baby

Feeding should be comfortable for you and your baby. Hold your baby fairly upright, with their head supported so they are able to swallow comfortably.

Place teat inside your baby's mouth, aim the teat to the roof of their mouth.
Lips should point outwards over the bottle.

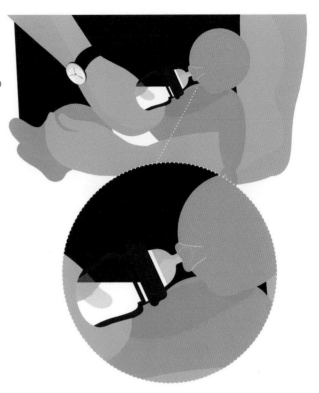

 CAUTION:
Never prop up your baby's bottle as they may choke on the milk.

Never leave them alone while feeding.

Keeping the teat full

To avoid your baby taking in air, always keep the teat full. If the teat becomes flattened while feeding, gently pull the corner of your baby's mouth to realise the suction.

 CAUTION:
When feeding always hold your baby in an upright position with their head slightly above their body to minimise the risk of chocking or getting an ear infection from milk running downwards into their ear.

Burping your baby

Your baby will need to be burped during a feed, once they have had enough, hold them upright and gently rub or pat their back to bring up wind.

Better out than in

Burping your baby

BUUUURRRRRP!

Get prepared: Burping

For first few months your baby will need to be burped during a feed as they may swallow air, which gets trapped in their stomach and can feel uncomfortable.

Burping will free up room in their stomach to avoid the feeling of false fullness and the urge to spit up their milk.

An indication that your baby may have wind is that they will squirm or raise their legs towards their stomach. Burping can be done half way through or at the end of a feed, but if your baby seems content and falls asleep during or after a feed, there is no need for burping.

Muslin cloth

Shoulder burp

Hold your baby using the shoulder hold. Follow step 1.

Repeat step 2 for five minutes. If your baby does not produce a burp within this time, proceed with feeding or clean up.

You can also hold your baby in an upright position that will help them to expel wind simply on their own.

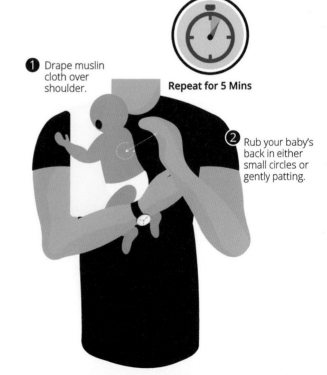

1 Drape muslin cloth over shoulder.

Repeat for 5 Mins

2 Rub your baby's back in either small circles or gently patting.

Sit up burp

Sit in a chair with your baby on your lap facing away from you. Follow step 1.

Repeat step 2 for five minutes. If your baby does not produce a burp within this time, proceed with feeding or clean up.

You can also hold your baby in an upright position that will help them to expel wind simply on their own.

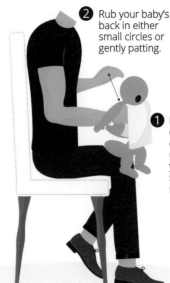

2 Rub your baby's back in either small circles or gently patting.

Repeat for 5 Mins

1 Drape muslin cloth over one hand and place on your baby's chest, under their chin. Lean your baby forward, supporting head and neck with your fingers.

Across your lap burp

Lay your baby, face down on your legs across your knees at a right angle to your body. Follow step 1.

Repeat step 2 for five minutes. If your baby does not produce a burp within this time, proceed with feeding or clean up.

Repeat for 5 Mins

2 Rub your baby's back in either small circles or gently patting.

1 Drape muslin cloth over your lap. Place your hand under your baby's chin and jaw to support head which should be held slightly higher than the rest of their body so blood doesn't rush to their head.

Babies with colic

Colic affects one in five babies. It usually begins within the first few weeks, and will often stop by four months old or the latest six months old.

It is a kind of stomach cramp that comes in waves that causes your baby to have crying outbursts which can last for several hours.

If your baby has colic this does not mean that they are unwell or that you are doing something wrong, the causes of colic are unknown and there is no clear evidence that colic has any long term effects. Your baby will continue to feed and gain weight normally.

The signs

The signs that your baby may have colic.

- Flushed face.
- Clenched fists.
- Knees drawn up towards stomach.
- Arched back.
- Seems distressed.
- Excessive, frequent crying.

Tips to help with colic

Different techniques to help your baby.

- Prevent them from swallowing air as much as possible.
- Comforting them when they are crying.
- Giving your baby a warm bath.
- Gently massaging your baby's tummy.

 TOP TIP!
Anti colic drops are available if your baby is suffering from colic.

Reflux

Reflux is when your baby brings up small amounts of milk which usually occurs when the valve that keeps the stomach contents down is not fully developed.

This is perfectly normal as long as your baby is showing no signs of discomfort and loosing weight. If they are vomiting regularly and bringing up a large amount of milk, and seem to be in discomfort while feeding, consult your health care professional.

By the age of twelve months most babies reflux symptoms disappear.

TOP TIP!
Anti reflux milk and medication are available if your baby is suffering from reflux. Consult your health care professional.

The signs

The signs that your baby may have reflux.

• Sudden crying.
• Irritability and pain.
• Frequent waking and poor sleep habits.
• Arching neck and back during or after feeding.
• Regurgitation or vomiting.
• Wet burp or frequent hiccups.

Tips to help with reflux

Different techniques to help your baby.

• Feeding little and often.
• Keeping your baby upright after a feed.
• Avoid dressing your baby in tight clothing around their stomach.

So fresh & so clean

Baby grooming from head to toe

Get prepared:
Baby bathing

Your new born baby will not need to have a bath for the first few weeks, but make sure you wash their face, neck, hands, and bottom every day. This is called "topping and tailing". Ideally products should not be used for the first few weeks, just warm water.

The best time to wash your baby is when they are awake and content, never straight after a feed, or when they are hungry or tired.

Small bathtub

Wash cloths

Towels

Hooded towels

Baby bath soap

Baby shampoo

Baby bath seat

Small cups or bowls

Baby comb

Fresh nappy

Cotton pads

Fresh clothing

Topping & tailing wash

TOP TIP!
Ensure the room temperature
is warm before
you begin.

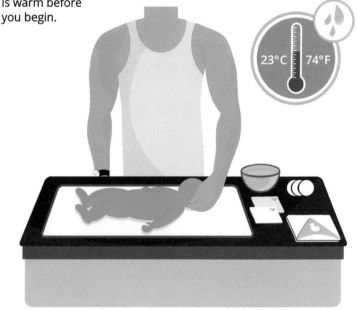

23°C 74°F

1. Lay your baby down on a changing mat.

2. Remove all their clothes, apart from their nappy. If your baby does not like the feeling of being completely undressed, keep their lower half wrapped in a dry towel.

3. Dip your cotton wool into the bowl of clean lukewarm water. Wipe gently around your baby's eyes, from the inner corner outwards. Use a fresh piece of cotton wool for each eye to avoid transferring infection.

4. Use a fresh piece of cotton wool to clean around ears. Wash the rest of your baby's face, neck and hands in the same way, and then dry gently with a towel.

5. Take off your baby's nappy, and wash your baby's bottom and genital area with fresh pieces of cotton wool. Dry carefully paying close attention to any creases in their skin.

6. Apply a fresh nappy and continue with dressing.

CAUTION:
Do not wash the umbilical stump.

Basin bath

TOP TIP!
Dip your elbow into the water to gauge the right temperature, if it is too hot for you, then it is too hot for your baby, re-adjust the temperature.

Always mix the water well, to avoid hot patches.

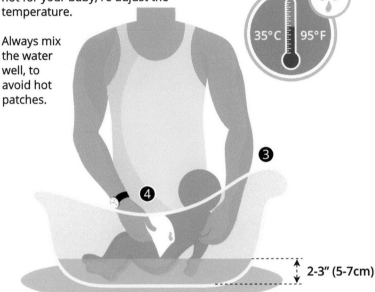

35°C | 95°F

2-3" (5-7cm)

❶ Before placing your baby into the bath, clean their face as described previously in the topping & tailing section, then while holding your baby support their head over the basin, wash their hair with shampoo, rinse carefully and dry gently.

❷ Remove nappy, wiping away any mess, lower your baby gently into the basin.

❸ Use one hand to hold under their upper arm and support their head and shoulders. With your other hand, use a wash cloth and soap to clean your baby. Rinse using a small cup filled with clean lukewarm water.

❹ Lift your baby out, pat them dry paying close attention to any creases in their skin.

CAUTION:
Never leave your baby unattended in the bath.

Always keep your baby's head above the water.

Bathing in a bath tub

At about six months your baby will be big enough to bath in a adult bath tub. A helpful product to use is a baby seat which will help your baby to balance easily without your assistance, therefore making it easier for you. Rubber bath mats can also be used but ensure assistance at all times. If your baby is reluctant to enter the bath tub, you can put toys in the bath to make things more fun for them to relax and enjoy their bath time.

35°C | 95°F

2-3" (5-7cm)

CAUTION:
Water level must be below your baby's waist.

Never leave your baby unattended in the bath.

TOP TIP!
Cover tap handles with specially designed covers to prevent your baby turning on the water or accidentally banging their head. A small towel may also be used.

Hair washing - Cradle cap

This is a skin condition that effects a
baby's scalp. It appears in the form of
yellow scales, and can sometimes extend
to the baby's face. Usually by the time
they are three months old it
will disappear.

To treat, Olive oil can be used as well as
cradle cap shampoos.

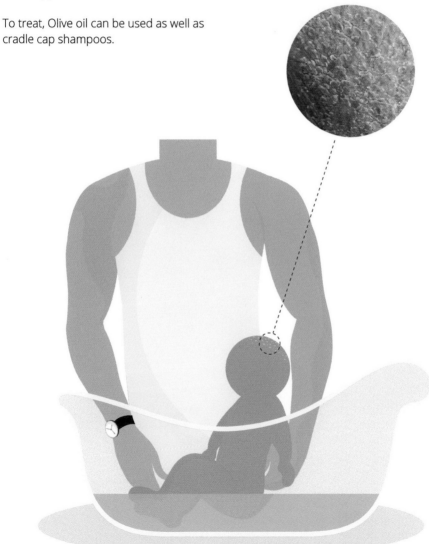

1
Apply Olive oil into the palms of your hands and onto your baby's scalp.

2
Massage the oil into the scalp for twenty seconds.

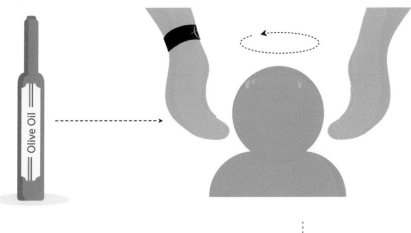

3
Wash your baby's head with a mild shampoo/cradle cap shampoo, you may need to wash your baby's head twice to remove all the Olive oil.

4
Rinse your baby's head thoroughly. Avoid getting water into their eyes or ears.

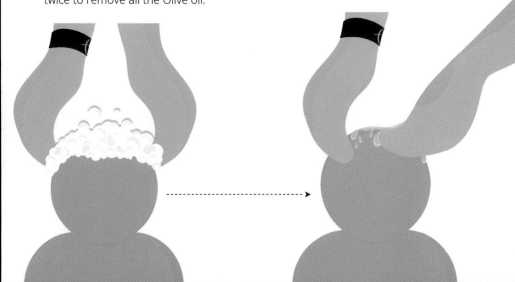

Use a soft baby brush to brush
away any loose scales.

 TOP TIP!
Style to preference!

 CAUTION:
Avoid scratching/picking off scales.

Get prepared:
Baby grooming

Grooming your baby can be done a little while before or after bathing, drying and dressing, as they may resist if you fuss with them too much at one time.

Grooming kit   Towels   Spray   Toy

Toothpaste and gauze   Cotton swab   Nail file   Nasal bulb

Cleaning nose
The cotton swab

Use a cotton swab, wet with a dab of water this will help to soften the mucus, then clean around your baby's nostrils.

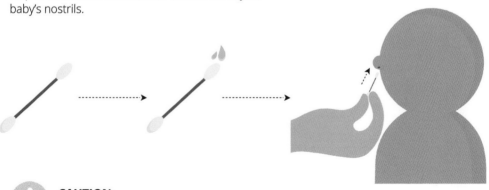

CAUTION:
Never insert the cotton swab inside the nostril.

Cleaning nose
The nasal bulb

The nasal bulb can help to clear a stuffy nose and make it easier for your baby to breathe, eat and sleep.

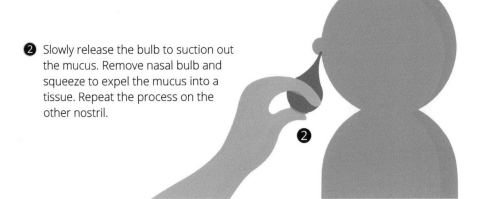

1 Squeeze the air out of the bulb to create a vacuum. Gently insert the tip into one nostril.

2 Slowly release the bulb to suction out the mucus. Remove nasal bulb and squeeze to expel the mucus into a tissue. Repeat the process on the other nostril.

TOP TIP!
Clean the bulb well with warm soapy water after each use. Place it tip side down in a glass to dry.

CAUTION:
This should be a gentle process. Never suction forcefully.

Cleaning ears
The cotton swab

Using a cotton swab, wipe away excess wax or dirt on the outside of the ear.

Water should not be allowed to enter your baby's ears as this may lead to infection.

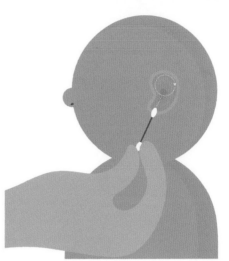

CAUTION:
Never place the cotton swab inside the ear canal.

Hair trimming

During the first year depending on your baby's hair growth, you may wish to trim their hair especially if it is growing down in front of their eyes.

1 Get assistance to help you with holding and distracting your baby.

2 Place a towel around your baby.

3 Cover your baby's eyes with one hand and dampen their hair with a spray of water.

4 Hold a section of hair with your index and forefingers and snip the hair with the scissors.

5 As your baby gets older and they need a hair cut rather than a trim, you can visit the barber or hair salon.

TOP TIP!
If your baby shows resistance, you may not be able to finish the job, so trim the longest hairs first. A toy is always a good distraction in order to help get the job done.

Nail trimming

Use clippers or nail scissors designed for babies. If your baby shows resistance rather use a nail file instead of cutting the nails with scissors. Always be careful not to nip your baby's skin.

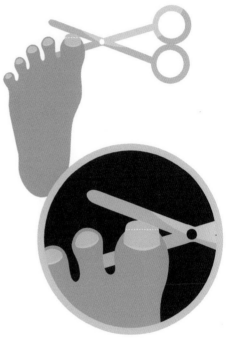

Cut your baby's finger nails as you would your own. File any sharp corners.

Cut your baby's toe nails straight across. File any sharp edges.

TOP TIP!
If your baby resists having their nails cut, wait for them to sleep as it will minimise the risk of injury.

Cleaning teeth/gums

Most baby's teeth will start to come through between the fourth and twelfth month.

In the early stages before your baby's teeth grow larger, a damp piece of gauze with a tiny smear of fluoride toothpaste can be used.

It is good to get your baby used to this process as it will become part of their daily routine.

1 Use a damp piece of gauze.

2 Use a children's fluoride toothpaste.

3 Wrap damp gauze around finger, apply a tiny smear of toothpaste and gently clean your baby's teeth/gums.

4 The easiest way to do this is to have your baby sitting on your knee.

 TOP TIP!
Not all babies will enjoy this, a toy can be used to distract them.

Small, soft toothbrushes are also available.

Siesta time

Putting your baby to sleep

Get prepared:
Sleeping setup

For the first six months, your baby should sleep in the same room as you, including their day time naps. In the early weeks your baby will find comfort in falling asleep either in your arms or when you are standing by the moses basket/cot.
As they get a bit older you can get them used to going to sleep without you comforting them, by putting them down before they fall asleep.

Your new born baby will have their own sleep pattern. Never compare your baby to another, as some babies sleep much more than others.

TOP TIP!
Place moses basket near to your bedside. This is convenient for night feeds as it is in arms reach.

Grow bags are available, which are a safer alternative to sheets and blankets. They keep your baby warm and cosy. The grow bag must be lightweight and be the right size fit for around your baby's neck.

Moses basket   Your bed   Bedside table

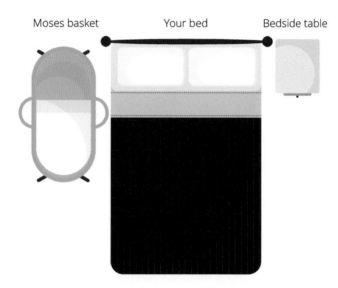

CAUTION:
Never sleep with your baby on a sofa or armchair. Sleeping with your baby in your bed can also be dangerous, you may roll over in your sleep and suffocate them, or they may roll out of your bed and be injured. Guard rails are available when your baby is old enough to sleep in a cot bed. Pillows should never be used as a guard rail.

The information from The Guidefather is advice only and not a substitute for examination, diagnosis or treatment by a qualified health professional.

64

Configuring your baby's room/nursery

Your baby's room should be set up and organised before they arrive. The following items shown in the diagram will help to make things easier for you and more comfortable for your baby.

Make sure you baby's room isn't too hot or too cold. This is very important, a temperature between 16 and 20 degrees is ideal for keeping them safe and comfortable.

TOP TIP!
Place your baby's cot in an area of the room that is visible from the door.

Ensure monitor, thermostat and night light are near to the cot.

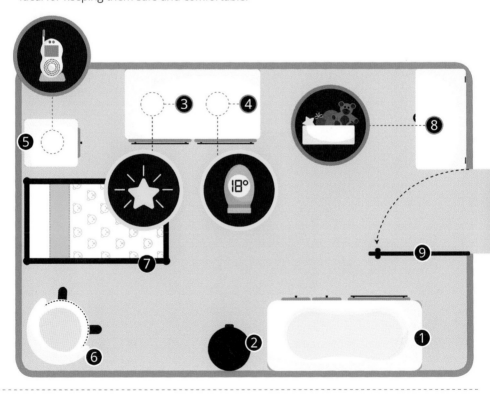

❶ Baby changing station	❻ Chair
❷ Nappy bin	❼ Cot
❸ Night light	❽ Toy box
❹ Room thermostat	❾ Door
❺ Monitor	

Helping your baby recognise day from night

It is good to teach your baby the difference between day time and night time.
Below are a few ways that can help them adapt to a normal sleep pattern.

Day time

- Open curtains/blinds.
- Turn on lights.
- Do not worry about every day noises.
- Play games/music.
- Wake your baby up for feeding

Night time

- Keep lights down low.
- Minimise noise.
- Talk quietly.
- Do not change your baby unless necessary.
- As soon as your baby has been fed, put them down.

TOP TIP!
Try to feed and entertain your baby later in the afternoon/ evening, so that they will sleep for longer during the night.

Settling your new born baby

One of the most common ways to help settle your baby, is to cradle them in your arms so that they are close to you.
Gently rock or sway your baby while singing or talking to them softly.

This method is ideal for the first few months, but a bed time routine is needed to prevent this becoming a habit of your baby falling asleep in your arms.

TOP TIP!
Try to sleep while your baby is sleeping during the day, this will help you, in case they are unsettled during the night.

Alternative ways of settling your baby

Methods that can be used.

- Warm bath to relax your baby.
- A Feed to help them feel content.

TOP TIP!
Try establishing a routine for your baby.

Bed time routine ideas

When your baby is around three months old, you may want to introduce a bed time routine. This will help to prevent sleeping problems later on. This is a good opportunity to spend some one-on-one time with your baby.

Here is an idea of a bed time routine.

Bathing your baby.

Changing into fresh nappy and clothes.

Brushing their teeth.

Laying your baby in their cot.

Reading a bed time story.

Dimming the lights.

Giving a goodnight kiss.

Singing a lullaby or putting on a musical mobile.

TOP TIP!
Once your baby is relaxed, leave the room while they are still awake, they will learn to fall asleep on their own.

Average hours of sleep

Newborn babies are asleep more than they are awake, they will wake during the night to be fed.

As your baby grows they will require fewer night feeds and will be able to sleep for longer periods of time during the night.

From 6 -12 months, night feeds may no longer be necessary therefore your baby may sleep up to twelve hours at night.

With your bedtime routine, your baby will be sleeping longer periods through the night with one or two naps during the day.

Baby's age	Average hours of sleep
Newborn	16 - 18 hours per day
3 - 6 months	14 - 15 hours per day
6 - 12 months	13 - 15 hours per day
12+ months	12 - 15 hours per day
2 years	11 - 12 hours per day

Disturbed nights

There are many reasons why your baby may be restless and wake during the night.

If your baby wakes, leave them for a few minutes and see if they settle back to sleep on their own. Resist the urge to pick them up straight away.

If they need comforting, changing or feeding ensure you do this in dim lighting and quietly to avoid fully awakening your baby.

Depending on symptoms of illness, comfort and treat as best you can, otherwise consult a health care professional.

Some reasons for disturbed sleep below.

TOP TIP!
If your baby uses a pacifier/ dummie for comfort, it is important to have a few spare at hand to replace one that may be lost or has fallen out of the cot.

| Too hot or too cold | Hungry | Dirty nappy |
| Teething | Growth spurts | Illness |

Sudden infant death syndrome (SIDS)

Sudden infant death syndrome (SIDS) is also known as cot death which is the sudden, unexpected and unexplained death of an apparently well baby.

Most deaths happen within the first six Months and infants born prematurely or with a low birth weight are at greater risk. It is also more common in baby boys.

SIDS is rare and the risk of your baby dying from it is low, so don't let worrying stop you from enjoying your baby's first few Months.

Most SIDS deaths occur while the child is asleep in their cot at night, however can also occur when they are asleep during the day or occasionally while they are awake.

The cause of SIDS is thought to be a combination of factors, it is not clear exactly what causes SIDS. It is believed that SIDS occurs at a particular stage and effects babies who are vulnerable to certain environmental stresses which include, tobacco smoke, getting tangled in bedding, a breathing obstruction or a minor illness.

It is thought that babies who die of SIDS have problems in the way they respond to these stresses, how they regulate their temperature, heart rate and breathing. Although no one knows exactly what causes SIDS, there are a few things you can do to reduce the risk.

Reduce the risk of cot death (SIDS)

- Place your baby on their back, for both day and night sleeps, in the same room as you for the first six months.

- Don't let anyone smoke in the same room as your baby, as being exposed to smoke can increase the risk of cot death.

- Don't share a bed with your baby, the safest place for them to sleep for the first six months is in a cot in the same room as you. Bed sharing increases the risk of your baby being suffocated or injured.

- Never sleep with your baby on a sofa or arm chair.

- Don't let your baby get too hot, as over heating can increase the risk of SIDS. If your baby is sweating or their tummy feels hot to touch, adjust their clothing/bedding.

- Don't let your baby's head become covered. If you choose to use light weight blankets place your baby in the "feet to foot" position which means that their feet are at the end of the crib, cot or pram, which will prevent them from wriggling down, under the blanket. Bedding should never reach higher than your baby's shoulders and should be securely tucked, so it can't slip over your baby's head. An alternative to blankets/bedding is a baby grow bag.

"Feet to foot"

- Although evidence is not strong, it is possible that using a dummie/pacifier at the start of any sleep period reduces the risk of cot death as it's believed to help with cardiac control.

How ya feeling?
Hot or cold?

Temperature check

The core temperature of your baby should be 36.4°C - (97.4°F).

A high temperature may indicate that your baby has an illness. If your baby has a raised temperature of 37.5°C or above it is usually considered to be a fever.

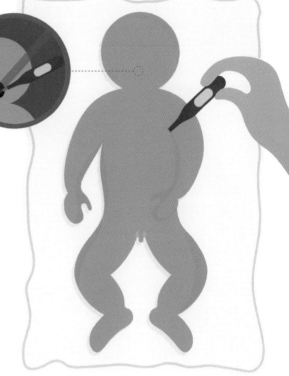

Signs of a fever:
- Feel hotter than usual to the touch.
- Feel sweaty or clammy.
- Have flushed cheeks.

If your baby has a raised temperature and signs of other illness, contact your health care professional.

TOP TIP!
The easiest way to check your baby's temperature is to use a thermometer under their armpit. Gently but firmly hold their arm against their body to keep the thermometer in place.

If their temperature is slightly above normal with no other symptoms, you can help to make them more comfortable and give them plenty to drink.

CAUTION:
Avoid taking your baby's temperature orally.

Layering your baby

Several light layers is the best way to dress your baby as you can adjust the clothing easily according to the temperature.

Your baby should wear one more layer than you find comfortable even if this is a blanket, as that counts as an extra layer.

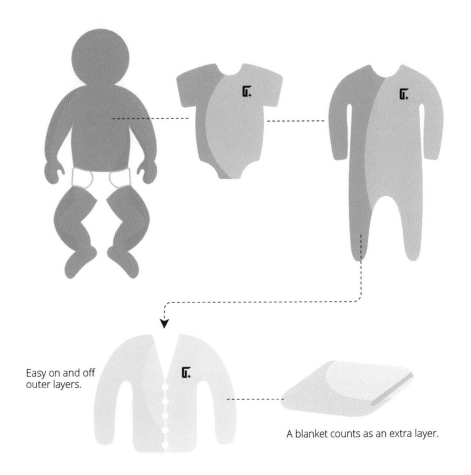

Easy on and off outer layers.

A blanket counts as an extra layer.

CAUTION:
Avoid dressing your baby too warmly.

TOP TIP!
Stretchy fabrics are easier to dress your baby.

Avoiding the cold

Several light layers should be worn as well as additional items such as hat, mittens, booties and a coat.

Even in winter try to keep your baby out of the sun, sunscreen should be used on any areas of skin that is exposed.

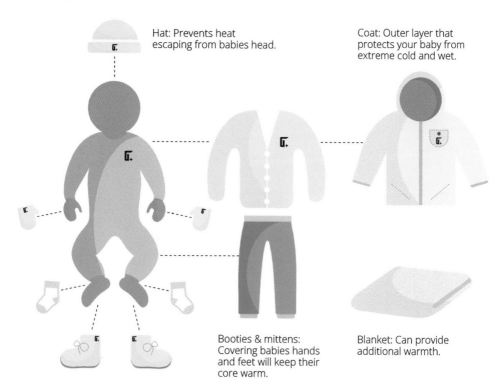

Hat: Prevents heat escaping from babies head.

Coat: Outer layer that protects your baby from extreme cold and wet.

Booties & mittens: Covering babies hands and feet will keep their core warm.

Blanket: Can provide additional warmth.

TOP TIP!
When going out, warm up your vehicle prior to placing your baby in the car seat.

Keep your baby's skin moisturised, cold wind outside can dry out their delicate skin.

Avoiding the heat

Clothing should be loose fitting cotton that is tightly woven, to prevent sunlight from passing through the fabric. Light coloured clothing is key to deflect sunlight.

To avoid your baby getting too hot, you must avoid direct sunlight and overdressing.

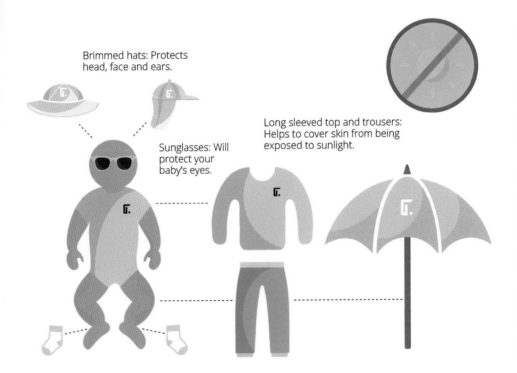

Brimmed hats: Protects head, face and ears.

Sunglasses: Will protect your baby's eyes.

Long sleeved top and trousers: Helps to cover skin from being exposed to sunlight.

Cotton Socks: Worn especially if your baby is in a stroller as their feet are more exposed
and susceptible to sunburn.

Umbrella/Parasol: Good for being attached to your pushchair and used for your baby to lay under.

CAUTION:
Avoid direct sunlight.

Appropriate Swimwear

Your newborns skin is very sensitive, the best way to avoid sunburn is to cover your babies skin as much as possible.

CAUTION:
Ensure all swim wear is UV Protected.

What'sa matta you?

Illness and first aid

Signs of illness

Crying can sometimes be a sign of illness, listen for a sudden change in the pattern or sound of your baby's cry. Symptoms such as a high temperature may also be a sign of illness. It may be something minor and treatable, if unsure contact your health care professional.

TOP TIP!
Always remain calm when your baby is crying.

CAUTION:
No matter how frustrated you become never shake your baby.

Looking after a sick baby

Looking after a sick child can be exhausting, getting as much rest/sleep when possible will help, and having someone to take over to give you a break will make things easier.

If the room temperature is too warm this will make your child feel worse, ensure the room is airy without being draughty or too cold.

Keeping them hydrated is key, so plenty to drink will help. If they are refusing food for the first day, nutritious drinks can be given. After that, tempt your child with a feed.

Try to comfort them as much as possible, and if they seem tired let them doze off when they need to.

Meningitis symptoms

There are two types of meningitis. Bacterial meningitis which is very serious and is a medical emergency, as it can cause severe brain damage and infect the blood. Viral meningitis is most common but less serious with mild flu like symptoms, it doesn't usually lead to blood poising.

Babies and young children under the age of five are most at risk of developing bacterial meningitis, particularly babies under the age of one years old.

Early symptoms of meningitis and septicemia (blood poisoning form of the disease) can be like other childhood illnesses, but babies will usually get ill quickly and get worse fast.

Not every baby gets all these symptoms. Symptoms can appear in any order.

Trust your instincts, if you think your baby has meningitis or septicemia, seek medical help immediately.

See next page for signs of symptoms.

TOP TIP!
The glass test - If you press the side of a clear glass firmly against the skin and the blotchy red rash does not fade or change colour, it's a possible symptom of bacterial meningitis.

Call your emergency services number

CAUTION:
If you notice any of the signs or symptoms of meningitis seek immediate medical help.

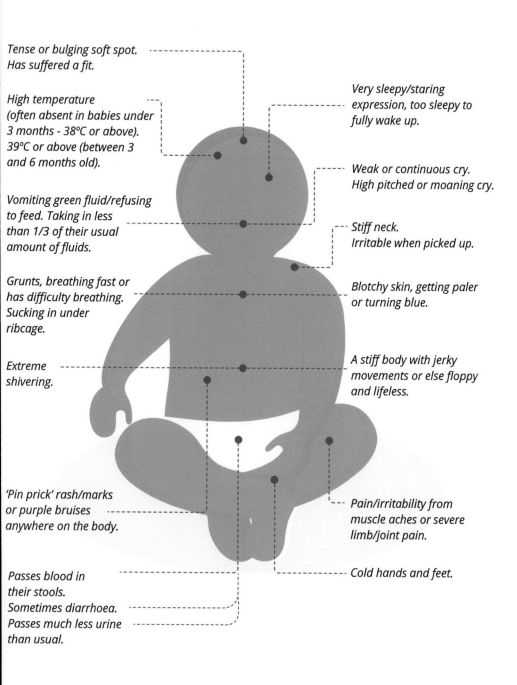

Tense or bulging soft spot. Has suffered a fit.

High temperature (often absent in babies under 3 months - 38°C or above). 39°C or above (between 3 and 6 months old).

Vomiting green fluid/refusing to feed. Taking in less than 1/3 of their usual amount of fluids.

Grunts, breathing fast or has difficulty breathing. Sucking in under ribcage.

Extreme shivering.

'Pin prick' rash/marks or purple bruises anywhere on the body.

Passes blood in their stools. Sometimes diarrhoea. Passes much less urine than usual.

Very sleepy/staring expression, too sleepy to fully wake up.

Weak or continuous cry. High pitched or moaning cry.

Stiff neck. Irritable when picked up.

Blotchy skin, getting paler or turning blue.

A stiff body with jerky movements or else floppy and lifeless.

Pain/irritability from muscle aches or severe limb/joint pain.

Cold hands and feet.

Vaccinations

Vaccinations protect your child against a range of serious and potentially fatal diseases, they will help fight against disease more effectively. Although it may be difficult to see your child being given an injection, they are quick and safe.

CAUTION:
Keep up to date with changes that may occur with vaccinations. Your health care professional can assist you with this.

Vaccination tips

- Clothing - easy to remove/roll-up. Thin cotton layers fastened with poppers are ideal.

- Stay Calm - your child may sense if you feel anxious. The procedure is quick and simple.

- Painkiller(if needed) - infant paracetamol or ibuprofen can be given if your child develops a mild fever (temp greater than 37.5°C) The area may be sore and red afterwards but the actual vaccination shouldn't hurt.

- Allergic reactions - this is rare, but if a serious allergic reaction (anaphylaxis) occurs, it will usually do so within minutes and the trained professional will be able to deal with this. Always inform the Doctor/Nurse of any previous reactions to vaccinations.

- Prone to fainting - this is rare, but if your child is prone to fainting, have them lay down for the vaccination.

Questions & Answers

Can parents refuse baby's vaccinations?
Yes, parents consent must be given.
If refused, it will be recorded. Evidence shows vaccinations do much more good than harm.

Missed vaccination appointment?
Make a new appointment, you can pick up immunisation schedule where it stopped rather than starting again.

Side effects?
Side effects include; a high temperate, temporary redness, swelling or tenderness on the area and a feeling of being unwell and irritated.

Is it painful?
It shouldn't hurt. If it does, it is quick and your baby may cry but will settle down after a few minutes.

Are vaccines needed before swimming?
You can take your baby swimming before or after their immunisations.

Any allergic reactions?
Allergic reactions are very rare, and are treatable. Signs of a reaction will occur within a few minutes. A rash or itching on part or all over their body will appear, the doctor or nurse will know how to treat this.
A severe reaction called anaphylactic shock, that causes difficulty breathing and sometimes collapsing can occur, however only happens about once in every million immunisations and is treatable. If an anaphylactic reaction has occurred to a previous dose, other doses shouldn't be given.

If baby is ill?
If your baby has a minor illness such as a cold, vaccinations should be given as normal. If they have a fever, wait until they have recovered.

Premature baby?
It is really important for premature babies to have vaccinations on time as they may be more at risk of catching infections.

Knowing when vaccinations are due?
Your doctors surgery/clinic will contact you automatically with an appointment when a vaccination is due.

First aid kit
Kit checklist

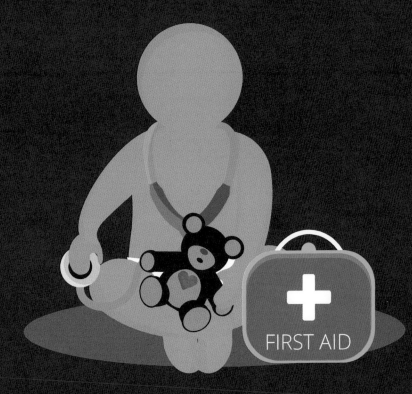

Incase of emergency

It is important to purchase or assemble a first aid kit to treat your baby in the event of an emergency. Two kits can be created, one for home use, and another that is portable to use while traveling. Ensure that the box is waterproof, easy to carry, and has a child proof lock on it.

TOP TIP!
Always take a first aid kit with you when traveling. Or create a smaller travel version. First aid training would be beneficial.

Sterile hand wipes

Medium and large
sterile dressing pads x2

Sterile gloves
x1 pair

Safety pins
x6

Antiseptic wipes x6
(Clean cuts and grazes)

Sterile eye pads x2
(Clear dirt, dust in eyes)

Tough cut scissors
x1 (Cut bandages)

Medicine dropper
x1

Thermometer
x1

Age appropriate
pain killers
(Soothes headaches
and fevers)

Tweezers
(Remove thorns,
splinters and
bee stings)

Calamine lotion
(Soothes rashes,
itching, chicken pox
and sunburn)

Waterproof plasters x1 pack
multiple sizes (Protects cuts,
blisters and sores)

Antihistamine cream
(Calms swelling, stings
and bites)

Correct bandages
x1 (Supports
strained joints)

Burn spray/
ointment

Triangular bandages
x4 (Slings)

CPR and heimlich maneuver
instruction card/manual and list
of emergency numbers.

FIRST AID ✚

CAUTION:
*Keep out of reach from children but in a easily
accessible place for adults. Replace out of date supplies.*

The information from The Guidefather is advice only and not a substitute for
examination, diagnosis or treatment by a qualified health professional.

86

Part III
Tiny tot to toddler

The fun begins...

From baby to toddler

The toddler transition

During the transition from baby to toddler your baby will become much more independent and will no longer depend on you for everything. They will learn, grow and reach many milestones. You will see changes in their physical growth, motor development and social skills.

Your baby's sleeping and eating habits will change, they will learn to walk, talk and use a potty.

TOP TIP!
Silence is always suspicious, always keep an eye on your toddler.

The information from The Guidefather is advice only and not a substitute for examination, diagnosis or treatment by a qualified health professional.

88

Safety First

Child proofing your home

Get prepared:
Child proofing

As your toddler becomes more mobile they will start to explore. Naturally they will sustain bumps and bruises which is normal, however child proofing your home will protect them from being seriously injured.

TOP TIP!
Child proof any other homes that your baby may visit i.e. Grandparents home.

General safety

Fire extinguisher

Handy to have as a solution to putting out a small fire.

Smoke alarm

Should be fitted on every level. Test batteries every week and change every year.

Carbon monoxide detector

Carbon monoxide can prove more harmful than smoke, because it is colourless, odorless and tasteless so this is an essential piece of child safety equipment.

TOP TIP!
Always practice an escape route in case of a fire in the home. Escape ladders are available.

The information from The Guidefather is advice only and not a substitute for examination, diagnosis or treatment by a qualified health professional.

90

Windows and blinds

Either cut or tie up curtain or blind cords. Ensure windows are locked and the key is in a safe, well known place. Window locks are available which will restrict how much space the window can open.

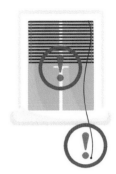

Doors

Door safety products are available which are designed to stop doors slamming on little fingers, as well as serious injury caused from the hinge side of the door.

 TOP TIP!
For fire safety fire-doors should always be shut at night.

Electricals

Cover electrical outlets and secure electrical cords. Unused electrical outlets can be covered with safety plug socket covers to prevent your toddler putting their fingers into the empty sockets. Dangling electrical cords should be secured to the wall or floor. Cable tidy units are available to keep cables neatly concealed.

Stairs

To protect your toddler, safety gates are available to install across staircases. They are also suitable for use in doorways and hallways to off-limit rooms. Most are suitable for children up to twenty four months.

 TOP TIP!
Always ensure safety gates are fastened securely to the wall or door frame.

Lounge area

Furniture

Furniture such as book cases must be secured to the wall, to prevent your toddler from pulling and toppling the furniture on to themselves. Furniture straps are available.

 TOP TIP!
Items placed on shelves or other furniture must be moved up a level out of reach, from your toddler.

Fireplaces and heaters

Fired guards can be fitted to all fires and heaters to prevent your toddler falling or reaching into fires. Radiator guards are also available to cover radiators to protect your toddler against heat from the radiator and also from any sharp edges.

Hot drinks

Do not leave hot drinks in easy reach places for your toddler as they will grab at cups and mugs that are left on low tables or on the floor.

Vacuum

Vacuum floors and carpets frequently to prevent your toddler from inhaling dirt or dust.

Bathroom

Bath tubs

Always put cold water into the bath first and then add the hot water ensuring that the temperature of the water is always tested before placing your toddler into the bath.

Taps

Tap straps and covers are available to prevent burns and scolds by preventing your toddler from turning on the taps and minimises injury against bumps on taps while in the bath.

Toilets

Toilet seat locks can be installed to prevent your toddler from playing in the toilet bowl which may contain cleaning chemicals.

The information from The Guidefather is advice only and not a substitute for examination, diagnosis or treatment by a qualified health professional.

93

Kitchen

Ovens

It is recommended that you keep your toddler out of the kitchen when cooking or baking. Locks can be fitted onto ovens, washers and dryers to prevent your toddler from opening these appliances. Oven door guards provide protection from the hot surface of your oven door.

Stoves

A safe way of cooking on the stove is to try and use the back burners. If the front burners are being used always keep the handles turned towards the rear of the stove. Stove guards are available to protect from scolds and burns. Stove knob guards can prevent your toddler from turning the stove on.

Cabinets

Cabinet locks can be fitted to prevent your toddler from opening draws and doors that may contain cleaning supplies, knifes, plastic bags, etc.

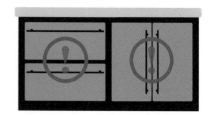

TOP TIP!
A baby safe draw with wooden spoons, small pots and pans, and plastic bowls can be created for your baby to explore and play safely.

Sharp objects

All sharp kitchen utensils should be either locked away safely or stored out of reach of children.

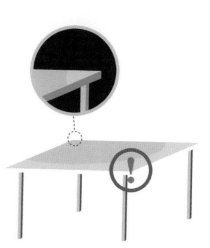

Tables

To protect your toddler from sharp corners of tables and shelves, corner cushions are available.

Table cloths

Remove table cloths as your toddler may pull on it and the items on the table may fall onto your toddler.

Buon appetito!

Weaning and solid foods

Get prepared:
Introducing solid foods

When your baby is around six months old they will be ready to start the weaning process onto solid foods.

Their digestive system would have had time to develop in order to cope fully with solid foods. It will also be easier for them to swallow properly at this age.

In the beginning the amount of food your baby takes is less important, as it is just getting them used to the idea of eating and exploring new flavors and textures. Your baby will still be getting most of their nutrition from either breast milk or infant formula.

The amount and variety of food your baby will eat will eventually increase so that they are eating the same foods as you, but smaller portions.

Giving your baby supplements in the form of vitamin drops which contain vitamins A, C and D will ensure your baby is getting the essential vitamins they need. Consult health care professional for more information.

TOP TIP!
Signs to show your baby is ready for solid foods.
1. Sitting upright and holding their head steady.
2. Coordination of eyes, hands and mouth to look at, pick up and put food into their mouth.
3. They can swallow their food rather than pushing it back out of their mouth.

CAUTION:
Always stay with your baby when they are eating, in case they start to choke.

For hot food always cool and test before serving to your baby.

Do not add salt or sugar to their food.

Baby high chair

Baby cutlery set

No-spill cup
1 year +

Bibs

Foods to avoid/restrict

Certain foods should be avoided as they may cause food allergies or make your baby ill. Others should be limited to a certain amount.

When you start to introduce some of these foods into your baby's diet, do so one at a time so you can spot any reaction. Ensure not to introduce any of these listed below before your baby is six months old.

Food allergy signs

Signs that your baby has a food allergy are:
- Diarrhoea or vomiting.
- Itchy throat and tongue.
- A cough.
- Wheezing and shortness of breath.
- Swollen lips and throat.
- Runny or blocked nose.
- Itchy skin or rash.
- Sore, red and itchy eyes.

CAUTION:
If you think your baby is having an allergic reaction to food, seek medical attention and advice.

Dairy

Raw/undercooked eggs

Citrus fruits

'Low fat' foods

Caffeine

Nuts

Honey

Sugar

First foods

Baby rice or cereal mixed with their usual milk can be given alongside with their breast milk or formula. Your baby's first foods should be soft cooked and mashed.

Fruit and vegetables that can be given include parsnip, potato, sweet-potato, carrot, apple and pear, ripe banana, peach, melon and avocado. Some of these can also be given as finger foods when your baby is ready for self feeding.

Second foods

These foods should still be soft cooked and slightly mashed.

Meats can be given such as chicken and fish (boneless) also pasta, noodles, rice, toast, hard boiled eggs, full fat dairy products such as yogurt, fromage frais and custard.

Cup and drinks

Introduce a cup, to give your baby sips of water to have with their meals. This will help your baby to learn how to sip rather than suck on a teat, which is better for their teeth. Water for babies over six months old does not need to be boiled.

Fruit juices must be diluted, one part juice to ten part water. Squashes/sugary fizzy drinks are not suitable for young babies, they contain sugar that can cause tooth decay. Tea and coffee is not suitable as it reduces amount of iron absorbed from food.

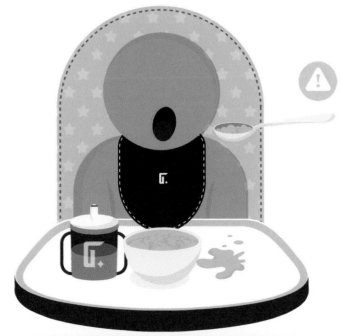

CAUTION:
Always secure your baby into the harness in their high chair.

Avoid giving your baby whole cows milk as a drink, until they are 1 year old.

Never force your baby to eat, if they refuse wait a few minutes and try again.

Alternative way of feeding

This is an alternative way of feeding your baby, sitting upright on your lap. If you are out and about and do not have access to a high chair, this way is ideal.

TOP TIP!
If out and about, be sure to place a cloth over your lap or arm to help keep your clothing clean from any spilt food.

Encourage self feeding

Before you get started, it is a good idea to either put a bib on, or undress your baby as it will get messy.

The self feeding process is slower, however is a wonderful learning experience. It will stimulate all of your baby's senses, from taste to smell, feeling textures and temperatures, and seeing the bright colours of all the different foods.

Your baby will play with their food which is part of learning about different foods. Always be patient and there to help if needed.

This process starts when your baby is around nine months old. They will use their forefinger and thumb to pick up food, this is called the 'pincer grasp'. At first give your baby easy dissolving finger foods, then as their chewing and swallowing ability improves introduce more textured foods such as, bread sticks, rice cakes, biscuits, toast, also cucumber sticks, cubes of cheese, pasta shapes and chopped fruits can be introduced.

Self feeding

Set out your baby's cutlery, this will get them familiar with handling them, even if they are not yet able to use them.

When your baby starts to feed themselves, try giving them sticky foods like porridge or mash that will not slide off their spoon before reaching their mouth.

You can help by placing the food onto the spoon and then allowing your baby to place the food into their mouth.

To speed up the process and ensure they are consuming enough, you can feed them a spoonful while they are concentrating on trying to feed themselves.

CAUTION:
Always check the temperature of your baby's food before serving it to them.

TOP TIP!
Place a spill mat under your baby's high chair in case any food ends up on the floor.

Buying a bowl that has a sucker on the bottom to stick to the high chair will stop the bowl ending up on the floor.

Always praise your baby as this will encourage them to keep trying and get better at self feeding.

Hollywood smile
Beware of the bite

Get prepared:
Teething

Your baby's first teeth will usually develop while they are still in the womb. Most babies start teething around six months old, however, this does vary, some do before four months old and some after twelve months old.

They will have all their milk teeth by the time they are two and a half years old.

Teething signs

Symptoms of teething include:
- Sore and red gums.
- One cheek is flushed.
- Dribbling.
- Chewing.
- Being fretful.

Teething rings

Teething gel

No-spill cup
1 year +

Medicine

Bibs

Muslin cloth

Dental care

Help your teething baby

Teething rings

A teething ring is safe for your baby to chew on. It will help ease any pain. Some teething rings can be placed in the fridge to become cool, which will help to soothe their gums.

 CAUTION:
Never place a teething ring into the freezer as it will become hard and may damage your baby's gums.

Teething gels

A teething gel that contains a mild local anesthetic can be used which will help numb any pain or discomfort, this should ideally be sugar free. Many contain antiseptic ingredients which help to prevent infection if there is any broken skin on the gums. This is for babies over four months old.

 CAUTION:
Teething gel must be specially designed for young children.

If your baby is under four months old discuss teething gel options with your health care professional.

Painkilling medicine

These medicines should ideally be sugar free and specially designed for children. They contain a small dose of paracetamol or ibuprofen to help ease pain. They can also be given to your baby if they have a raised temperature.

CAUTION:
Always follow dosage instructions that come with the painkilling medicine.

Aspirin should not be given to children under sixteen years old.

Cool drinks

A cool drink will help to soothe your baby's gums. The best option is cool water, as it is sugar free.

CAUTION:
Always ensure the drink is not too cold.

TOP TIP!
Raw fruit and vegetables are ideal for your baby to chew when teething. Always supervise your baby in case they choke.

Comforting and playing with your baby will help distract them from teething pain.

Frequently wiping dribble from their chin will help prevent a rash from developing.

The teething process
Milk teeth

These usually develop while your baby is growing in the womb, they will start to emerge through the gums when your baby is around four to six months old. This is known as teething.

Incisors
Bottom front teeth

At around five to seven months, these will be the first teeth to come through your baby's gums.

Incisors
Top front teeth

These will come through at around six to eight months.

Top lateral Incisors
Either side of top teeth

At around eleven months the top lateral incisors will come through.

Bottom lateral Incisors
Either side of bottom front teeth

From ten to twelve months the bottom lateral incisors will come through.

Molars
Back teeth

These will come through at about twelve to sixteen months.

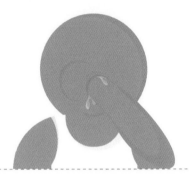

Canines
Towards the back of mouth

These will come through at around sixteen to twenty months.

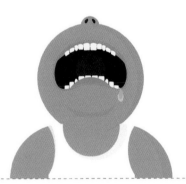

Second molars

Finally these come through at around twenty to thirty months. Your baby will then have all of their milk teeth.

Brushing teeth

When your baby's teeth start to come through you can use a baby tooth brush with a tiny smear of children's fluoride toothpaste to brush them.

It may be difficult to brush them properly at first but getting your baby used to the process and into a routine is important. This must be done twice a day.

CAUTION:
Minimise sugar intake as this will cause tooth decay.

TOP TIP!
To make the process easier, make brushing your baby's teeth into a game. Brushing your teeth at the same time will help encourage your baby to do the same.

Taking your baby to the dentist when you have a dental appointment will get them used to the idea, making it less daunting when they are ready for a check up.

Always praise your baby as this will encourage them to brush their teeth daily.

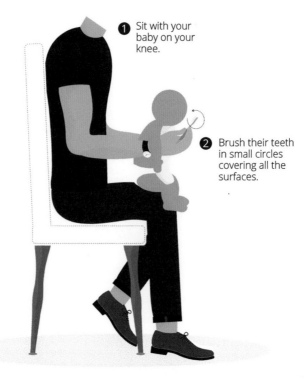

1. Sit with your baby on your knee.

2. Brush their teeth in small circles covering all the surfaces.

Doing the business

Potty training like a pro

Get prepared: Potty training

Always remember, never compare your baby with others, every child is different and will use the potty when they are ready. This must not be forced but always encouraged.

Potty training should start around eighteen to twenty four months.

The signs

The signs that your baby may be ready:
- Your baby will know that they have a wet or dirty nappy.
- They may tell you when they are doing their business in their nappy.
- They will let you know in advance when they need to go.

Potty

Training loo seat

Toilet step

Wipes

Pull up pants

Big kid pants

Hand soap/sanitiser

Waterproof mattress sheets

Starting potty training

First things first, explaining the process of using a potty will help your toddler to understand what they need to do and what the potty is used for.

It is a good idea to have more than one potty placed around your home so that one is near by at all times to avoid any accidents.

At first removing your toddlers nappy and sitting them on the potty regularly will help get them used to it. Also asking them regularly if they need to use the potty, will help remind them that it is there to use.

If they have an accident, do not make a fuss as this will make your toddler feel anxious and worried, which will dishearten them for next time. Having an accident will let them experience the feeling of standing or sitting in a puddle of wee, so will hopefully encourage them to use the potty when they have not got a nappy on.

When your toddler does succeed, ensure praise is always given. They will feel proud of themselves.

Remember you can always go back to nappies for a few weeks and try again. They will eventually want to be dry.

 TOP TIP!
Using charts or a potty card with stamps or stickers, will encourage your toddler to use the potty. For example, twelve successful potty visits amount to twelve stickers or stamps, that will then result in a surprise for your toddler.

Letting your toddler choose their big girl or boy pants will get them excited to get rid of their nappy.

Little Joe's Potty Chart

12 ⭐ = Surprise

Out and about potty training

When out and about it is a good idea to take a potty in the car, this can be taken into the toilet for them to use. If your journey is long distance, and toilet breaks are not as frequent, training pull-ups can be worn to avoid any mishaps. Always carry a change of clothing, because it is unpleasant for your toddler to sit in wet or dirty clothes.

TOP TIP!
Placing a changing pad on your toddlers car seat, will help keep it dry in case they have an accident.

Staying dry through the night

Once your toddler has achieved daytime dryness, getting them dry through the night can start. Cut back on fluids towards the evening, and avoid drinks that contain caffeine before bed time. Encourage your toddler to use the potty before getting into bed. When you notice their nappy is dry in the morning you can start putting them to bed without a nappy.

If your toddler wets the bed during the night, reassure them that mistakes happen and the sheets can be washed, although this can be messy and frustrating always stay calm as they will eventually get the hang of staying dry throughout the night.

TOP TIP!
Use a waterproof protective mattress cover.

It's a good idea to place a potty next to their bed with a night light near by, in case they need to use it during the night.

From potty to toilet

Once your toddler has mastered using a potty they may want to start using an adult toilet. Using a training loo seat and a toilet step, will help until your toddler is big enough to use it without.

The information from The Guidefather is advice only and not a substitute for examination, diagnosis or treatment by a qualified health professional.

112

Temper tantrums
Taming your toddler

Get prepared:
Temper tantrums

The only way you can get prepared for temper tantrums is to try and understand why your toddler is having a tantrum and to think of different strategies to help them cope, calm them down or distract them.

Tantrums usually start around eighteen months and are very common. The main reason your toddler will have a tantrum is because of frustration. Your toddler will find it difficult to communicate and express themselves, therefore becoming increasingly frustrated.

In certain situations there may be a simple solution, such as; if they feel tired, let them sleep, if they feel hungry, let them snack and if they want attention, show them love.

Once your child can talk they will be less likely to have tantrums and by the age of four, they will be much less common.

The signs

The signs of a temper tantrum:
- Crying or whining.
- Kicking legs.
- Throwing fists.
- Hitting or biting.
- Throwing objects or themselves to the floor.

TOP TIP!
Always stay calm.

What's the reason?

There are a number of different reasons why your toddler may be having tantrums. Trying to establish the reason for the change in their mood will help you come to a resolution easier.

Below are some examples:
- Birth of a new baby, change of child minder, moving house starting a new playgroup or class.

- Noticing upset or tension caused from problems within the family.

- Phase of being upset or insecure.

- Getting a reaction and attention.

- Your child may be tired, bored, hungry, over excited or frustrated.

Temper tips

Try to understand what your toddler is wanting to express. Talking to them calmly and finding out what is the problem, can help to avoid a tantrum before it starts.

If you feel they are showing signs of having a tantrum, distract them in order to divert their attention to something else.

Do not lose your temper or shout back at your child, try to stay calm. Reacting will only teach them that their behavior gets a reaction from you. Talking calmly will show them the right way to communicate, children mimic what they see.

Do not give into your child, as this will create long term problems, as they will learn that a tantrum will get them what they want.

Avoid bribing with sweets or treats.

To encourage good behavior praise your child with clapping, smiling and plenty of cuddles.

When you're out and about, i.e. shopping, if your toddler has a tantrum it can be embarrassing, which will make it harder to stay calm. To avoid this try and involve your child in the process by letting them help you with your shopping.

Hitting, biting and kicking may be a way that your toddler reacts when they are having a tantrum. They may not understand that this hurts and rather than retaliating, let them know calmly but firmly that it is not acceptable and you will not allow it.

Letting your child run and shout at the park will help release frustration in a way that is not hurting anyone else.

Difficult behavior

There is no such thing as a perfect parent or a perfect child, both will have bad days which can make it hard to get on well together all day, every day.

It can be hard for a parent when you are tired or stressed, and your child is being difficult, even the smallest thing can make you angry.
Sometimes their behaviour can become worse, especially if they know that they are making you angry or upset, which will then make you feel even worse and create a vicious cycle. If you know they are wanting a reaction, ignore their bad behavior.

Most people will experience difficult behavior when it comes to dressing, eating, bathing or going to bed.

Dealing with difficulty

Below are ways to help you deal with your toddlers difficult behavior.

- Change their routine. When performing particular tasks that cause difficult behavior, changing the time or way in which you do this can help stop the difficult behavior. It may be that they are tired, hungry or not feeling well.

- Quality time together. Fun activities that can be enjoyed together, will show your child that a happy parent is more fun than an angry parent. Their daily routine of dressing, eating etc, can also be made fun to encourage cooperation instead of resistance.

- Discipline when necessary. Don't let telling off your child become a habit, only do so when it matters. Doing this will have more impact, making them realise that they are doing wrong.

- Be prepared to apologise. If you have lost your temper because of being tired or stressed, saying sorry will make you both feel better.

- Leading by example. Your behavior has an effect on your child, show them how to behave.

- Active child. If your child is active and always wanting to learn and explore, let them do this as much as possible, but in the safest way.

- Take care. Dealing with a child with difficult behavior can be exhausting, having an early night or talking to someone about it can help.
Take care of yourself in order to take care of them.

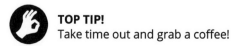

TOP TIP!
Take time out and grab a coffee!

Work hard, play harder

Play, learning and speech

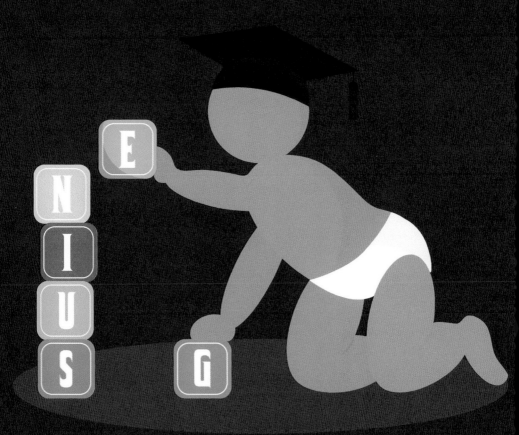

Get prepared:
Development

As your toddler grows they will require time and attention in order to develop. All children love to play which is the most effective way for them to learn. Everything your toddler looks at, thinks about, and does is part of the learning process. They need to explore, discover and experiment. Talking about anything and everything will help them to pick up lots of new words.

Playing can help them to learn everyday skills that they will need to know as they get older. For example, tidying up toys while singing or dancing makes it fun for them, as well as teaches them to be responsible for clearing up after themselves. Letting your toddler get involved with tasks that allow them to copy what you do, is another great way for them to learn different skills.

TOP TIP!
Only allow your toddler to have a couple of hours of T.V/tablet time per day.

Books

Cooking utensils

Paint brushes

Pencils/crayons

Costumes

T.V/tablets

Ideas for play

Playing with water

Toddlers love playing with water, whether it is in the bath, paddling pool, or using plastic bowls. They will enjoy pouring water into cups, splashing, squirting and making bubbles.

It is great for teaching them about warm and cool water, and objects that float and sink.
It will also teach them everyday skills such as, washing up.

 TOP TIP!
Keep towels handy in case of any spilt water that may be dangerous on floors.

 CAUTION:
Always supervise your toddler when they are playing around water as they can drown in only two inches of water.

Drawing and painting

Using chunky wax crayons will make it easier for them to hold at first, supply a large piece of paper in order for your toddler to scribble freely.

Drawing different pictures for your toddler will keep them interested and help learn different shapes, animals, etc. They will then go onto using felt tip pens and pencils, and will eventually try to copy what you draw.

 TOP TIP!
In case of mess either undress or dress your toddler in old clothes and cover surrounding area with a protective sheet.

Getting creative

Making pictures by gluing and sticking different materials and textures such as foil, ribbon or string will help your toddler express their creativity. Your toddler may also enjoy molding play dough.

CAUTION:
Ensure glue is non toxic, washable and safe.

Using their imagination

Blocks and building toys, dress up clothes and props are the best toys to encourage your toddler to use their imagination.

Outdoor play

Outdoor play helps your toddler to burn off energy, as well as helping their coordination and balance.

It is a good learning opportunity to discover different things for example, shadow tracing, collecting twigs and leaves and discovering outdoor creatures.

CAUTION:
Always supervise your toddler when outdoors.

Speech

From around six months your baby will make certain sounds that are easier to pronounce such as 'da' 'ba' or 'ma'. If you repeat these sounds and smile, showing enthusiasm, this will encourage them to continue imitating you.

Around twelve months old they will begin to use one or more words such as 'mamma' or 'dadda'. Naming and pointing at things will help them to learn words and they will eventually start to copy what you say.
If they say the word incorrectly at first, repeat the word correctly rather than telling them off for getting the word wrong. They will be able to recognise certain objects even if they are not able to name them and may also be able to understand and follow simple instructions.

From eighteen to twenty-four months they may use between twenty to fifty, or more, simple single words and may start to put two or more words together.
They may also be able to understand words sometimes as many as two-hundred to five-hundred words.

Reading books, singing songs and teaching them nursery rhymes will help your toddler to develop language and communication skills. At this point a couple of hours of television a day is suitable as it will help with the learning process.

Reading to your toddler will get them familiar with sounds, rhythms and how language flows together.

If you are worried about your child's language development talk to your health care professional.

 CAUTION:
If your toddler is using a pacifier/ dummy, restrict its use to sleep time as it is hard to learn to talk with a dummy.

...And that's that!

You're ready

You now have the fundamental basics and understanding to help prepare yourself for the first couple of years of parenthood. Utilise the Top Tips and keep an eye on the things to be cautious of. Put all into practice and you'll be sure to succeed.

Enjoy the journey!

"A man who doesn't spend time with his family,can never be a real man" -

Vito Corleone, The Godfather Movie, 1972

Follow **The Guidefather** Now

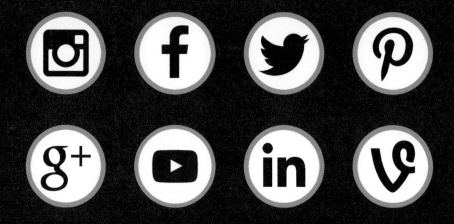

A guide to fathering
'Information you can't refuse'